Chapter 1:

Why Urban Sustainability Matters

The Urban Carbon Footprint

Urban areas are the engines of economic growth, innovation, and culture, but they are also the largest contributors to global environmental challenges. Cities house over 55% of the world's population and consume more than 75% of natural resources.

Urban centers generate 70% of greenhouse gas emissions due to transportation, energy consumption, and waste management practices. For example, the average urban household produces nearly double the waste compared to rural counterparts. Addressing these issues in densely populated areas is essential to achieving global sustainability goals.

Common Misconceptions About Sustainability in Cities

Myth 1: Sustainable living is only for rural areas. Many people believe that eco-friendly practices, like gardening or composting, require ample space only available in rural areas. However, innovations like vertical gardens and compact compost bins prove this wrong.

Myth 2: Urban areas lack resources for sustainability. Cities often have more accessibility to green products, recycling centers, and public transport than rural areas.

Myth 3: Individual efforts don't matter in cities. While it's true that systemic change is needed, individual actions, such as reducing energy use or supporting local eco-initiatives, create a ripple effect that inspires broader community shifts.

The Benefits of Urban Sustainability

1. Health Benefits:

Cleaner air from urban greenery and reduced car use.

Access to fresh produce through urban gardening.

2. Financial Benefits:

Lower energy bills from efficient appliances and insulation.

Savings from reduced consumption and DIY solutions.

3. Community Benefits:

Stronger connections formed in sustainability groups.

Improved mental health due to greener, calmer environments

Overcoming Challenges in Urban Sustainability

1. Space Constraints:

Use multi-functional furniture and wall-mounted storage to optimize space for eco-projects.

Convert small balconies into productive gardens with tiered planters.

2. Time Constraints:

Incorporate small, quick habits, like switching off lights or choosing reusable items.

3. Resource Availability:

Seek local green markets and co-ops for affordable eco-friendly goods.

Use free community programs, such as workshops on composting or solar panel subsidies.

How This Guide Can Help

This book is structured to guide you step-by-step in transforming your lifestyle into one that aligns with urban sustainability goals. Chapters progress from basic habits to advanced strategies.

Practical tips are tailored for city living, addressing common challenges like space and time constraints.

Case studies and success stories demonstrate that sustainable living is achievable, no matter the circumstances.

Together, we'll explore ways to make your urban environment greener and healthier while inspiring others in your community to follow suit. Remember: every small action contributes to a global movement toward sustainability.

Chapter 2:

Getting Started with Sustainable Living

Assessing Your Current Lifestyle

Before making changes, it's crucial to understand where you currently stand. Conduct a sustainability audit of your lifestyle by considering the following:

- ✓ Energy Use: Check your monthly electricity and water bills. Are there areas where consumption can be reduced?

- ✓ Waste Habits: Track your household waste for a week. How much is recyclable? How much is food waste?

✓ Shopping Patterns: Evaluate your purchases. Are they frequently disposable, non-recyclable, or unnecessary?

Exercise:

Create a journal to document your observations. For example:

✓ Energy: Left lights on in three rooms today.
✓ Waste: Threw away leftovers twice this week.

This exercise will provide a baseline for improvement.

Sustainability Audit Journal

Week of: [Insert Date]

Section 1: Energy Use

- **Electricity Bill:**
    - Amount this month: _______
    - Average usage (kWh): _______
    - Observations:
        - [e.g., Lights left on in unused rooms, high energy use from appliances.]
    - Potential Changes:
        - [e.g., Replace bulbs with LEDs, use power strips to reduce standby power.]

- **Water Bill:**
    - Amount this month: _______
    - Average usage (liters): _______
    - Observations:
        - [e.g., Long showers, dripping taps.]
    - Potential Changes:
        - [e.g., Install low-flow showerheads, repair leaks.]

Section 2: Waste Habits

- **Type and Volume of Waste (Track for 7 Days):**

-

Day	Recyclables (kg)	Food Waste (kg)	General Trash (kg)	Observations & Notes
Day 1	_________	_________	_________	[e.g., Too many single-use plastics.]
Day 2	_________	_________	_________	[e.g., Unused vegetables spoiled.]
...				
Day 7	_________	_________	_________	

- **Overall Observations:**
    - [e.g., 40% of waste was recyclable but not sorted. Consider a better sorting system.]
    - Potential Changes:
        - [e.g., Set up a compost bin, switch to reusable grocery bags.]

Section 3: Shopping Patterns

- **Track Purchases for the Week:**

Item	Category	Reusable/Disposable	Necessary?	Notes
[e.g., Pack of water bottles]	Convenience Item	Disposable	No	Look for a refillable option.
[e.g., Groceries]	Food	Mix	Yes	Choose less packaged items.
[e.g., New clothing]	Apparel	Reusable	No	Impulse buy—avoid next time.

- **Reflections:**
    - [e.g., Too many non-essential purchases. Plan better before shopping.]
    - Potential Changes:
        - [e.g., Make a list before shopping, choose second-hand items.]

Section 4: Goals for Next Week

- Reduce electricity usage by _______%.
- Compost _______% of food waste.
- Purchase only _______ non-essential items.

Weekly Reflections

- What worked well this week?
    - [e.g., Remembered to turn off lights more consistently.]
- What needs improvement?
    - [e.g., Still throwing away food scraps—need to set up a compost bin.]

Setting Realistic Goals

Goals should be both achievable and impactful. Use the SMART framework:

- Specific: Decide on exact actions, such as reducing single-use plastic by 50%.

- Measurable: Track progress with quantifiable metrics, like monthly energy usage.

- Achievable: Start with manageable steps, such as bringing reusable bags to the store.

- Relevant: Ensure goals align with your priorities, like saving money or reducing waste.

- Time-Bound: Set deadlines, like achieving a 10% reduction in electricity use within three months.

Example Goal:

"I will compost kitchen scraps to reduce food waste by 30% within the next two months."

Understanding Your City's Resources

Many cities offer programs and incentives to support sustainable living. Here's how to find and utilize them:

- ✓ Recycling Centers: Research local facilities that accept paper, glass, and electronic waste.
- ✓ Green Incentives: Check for government rebates on solar panels or energy-efficient appliances.
- ✓ Workshops and Classes: Join free or low-cost sessions on composting, urban gardening, or upcycling.
- ✓ Community Resources: Libraries often lend tools for DIY projects, reducing the need to buy new ones.
- ✓ Pro Tip: Subscribe to your city's sustainability newsletter for updates on local initiatives.

Small Changes, Big Impact

Starting small can make sustainability feel less overwhelming. Here are some beginner-friendly actions:

1. Switch to Reusables: Replace disposable water bottles, straws, and bags with reusable alternatives.
2. Opt for Energy-Efficient Lighting: LED bulbs use up to 75% less energy than traditional bulbs.
3. Unplug Devices: Electronics on standby still consume power. Plug them into power strips for easy disconnection.
4. Plan Meals: Avoid food waste by planning weekly meals and using leftovers creatively.
5. Choose Public Transport: Reduce emissions by taking buses, subways, or carpooling whenever possible.

Even one small change, like turning off lights when not in use, can create a ripple effect of positive habits.

Creating a Sustainability Action Plan

An action plan will help you stay organized and committed. Follow these steps:

1. Define Your Objectives: What areas do you want to improve? For example:

- ✓ Reduce household waste.
- ✓ Lower water usage.

2. Break It Into Steps:

- ✓ Short-Term (1 month): Start recycling plastics and paper.
- ✓ Medium-Term (3 months): Begin composting food scraps.
- ✓ Long-Term (1 year): Install water-saving fixtures.

3. Track Progress:

- ✓ Use apps like "JouleBug" or spreadsheets to monitor habits and savings.
- ✓ Celebrate milestones, like reducing waste by 10% in the first month.

4. Adapt and Refine: Adjust goals based on challenges or new opportunities.

To sum up, by assessing your current habits, setting achievable goals, and taking small steps, you're laying the foundation for a sustainable lifestyle. Every journey begins with a single step, and your efforts—no matter how small—are a crucial part of a larger movement toward a healthier planet.

Chapter 3:

Urban Gardening

Starting Your Balcony Garden

Urban gardening is an excellent way to reduce your environmental footprint and reconnect with nature, even in limited spaces like balconies or rooftops.

Step-by-Step Guide to Begin:

    a. Assess Your Space: Measure your balcony or windowsill and identify areas that receive sunlight. Most vegetables and herbs need at least 4-6 hours of sunlight daily.

b. Choose the Right Containers: Opt for lightweight pots, hanging baskets, or recycled containers. Ensure they have proper drainage holes.

c. Select Your Soil: Use organic potting soil with added compost for maximum nutrients.

d. Plan Your Layout: Arrange plants vertically or in tiers to make the most of your space.

Beginner-Friendly Plants for Balcony Gardens:

* Herbs: Basil, mint, parsley.
* Vegetables: Cherry tomatoes, lettuce, radishes.
* Fruits: Strawberries, dwarf citrus trees.

Pro Tip: *Use a water tray beneath pots to prevent water from dripping onto neighbors' balconies.*

Vertical Gardening Techniques

Vertical gardening is ideal for maximizing space in urban settings. This technique allows plants to grow upwards rather than outwards, making it perfect for walls, fences, or small balconies.

Ideas for Vertical Gardening:

1. Trellises: Ideal for climbing plants like beans, cucumbers, and peas.

2. Wall Planters: Install racks or pockets on walls for herbs and flowers.

3. Hanging Planters: Use hooks or railing planters for strawberries, spinach, or cascading flowers.

4. Repurposed Materials: Turn old pallets, ladders, or shoe organizers into creative vertical gardens.

Benefits of Vertical Gardening:

- Saves space while increasing yield.
- Improves air quality and reduces heat absorption on building walls.
- Creates a visually appealing green space.

Maintenance Tip: *Regularly check for pests and ensure even watering to prevent dehydration.*

Growing Herbs, Vegetables, and Flowers

Herbs:

- Herbs are easy to grow and highly rewarding for urban gardeners.
- Light Needs: Place herbs like basil, thyme, and oregano in a sunny spot.
- Watering: Water lightly but consistently. Overwatering can rot roots.
- Harvesting: Regularly trim herbs to encourage growth and prevent flowering.

Vegetables:

- Vegetables like lettuce, radishes, and cherry tomatoes thrive in small spaces.
- Containers: Use deep pots for root vegetables like carrots.
- Soil: Ensure soil is rich in organic matter.
- Growth Time: Choose fast-growing varieties to maximize output.

Flowers:

- Flowers not only beautify your space but also attract pollinators.
- Shade-Loving Flowers: Begonias, ferns, and impatiens work well in low-light conditions.
- Sun-Loving Flowers: Petunias, marigolds, and geraniums thrive in bright spaces.

Tip for Success: *Group plants with similar sunlight and watering needs for easier maintenance.*

Community Gardens

If you lack balcony or rooftop space, joining a community garden is a great alternative. These shared spaces allow urban residents to cultivate plants collaboratively.

How to Join or Start a Community Garden:

1. Research Existing Gardens: Look for local initiatives through websites or social media groups.

2. Contact Local Authorities: Request unused plots of land for gardening purposes.

3. Collaborate with Neighbors: Gather a group of like-minded individuals to share resources and labor.

Benefits of Community Gardens:

- ✓ Access to larger plots for growing a variety of crops.
- ✓ Opportunities to learn gardening techniques from others.
- ✓ Strengthened community ties and social interaction.

Example: *In New York City, the GreenThumb program provides materials and support for over 600 community gardens.*

Overcoming Challenges in Urban Gardening

Challenge 1: Limited Sunlight

Solution: Use reflective surfaces like mirrors to redirect light. Choose shade-tolerant plants like spinach and lettuce.

Challenge 2: Lack of Space

Solution: Opt for compact, high-yield plants like microgreens or dwarf varieties of fruit trees.

Challenge 3: Pests

Solution: Create natural pest repellents using neem oil or garlic spray. Introduce beneficial insects like ladybugs to control harmful pests.

Challenge 4: Watering Issues

Solution: Install a drip irrigation system or use self-watering pots to ensure consistent hydration.

Challenge 5: Weather Extremes

Solution: Use frost covers during cold months and shade nets during hot summers to protect plants.

Urban gardening transforms even the smallest spaces into productive, sustainable havens. Whether you're growing herbs on a windowsill or joining a community garden, every plant you nurture contributes to a greener, healthier urban environment.

Chapter 4:

Waste Reduction in Small Spaces

Decluttering for Sustainability

Decluttering your home is the first step toward reducing waste. A minimalist lifestyle not only creates a cleaner space but also ensures that items are used purposefully.

Steps to Declutter Sustainably:

1. Sort and Categorize: Separate items into four categories: Keep, Donate, Recycle, and Repurpose.

2. Avoid Throwing Away Usable Items: Donate clothes, books, or appliances to local charities or secondhand stores.

3. Repurpose Old Items: Transform jars into storage containers, or old T-shirts into cleaning rags.

4. Adopt a "One In, One Out" Rule: For every new item you buy, remove an old one to maintain balance.

Tip for Success: *Focus on quality over quantity. Invest in durable, versatile items to avoid frequent replacements.*

Composting in Apartments

Composting is a powerful way to reduce food waste and create nutrient-rich soil. Even in small spaces, composting is manageable with the right tools.

Methods for Apartment Composting:

1. Bokashi Composting:

- ✓ A Japanese method that ferments food scraps using a special bran.
- ✓ Requires an airtight container and is odorless.

2. Vermicomposting:

- ✓ Uses worms to break down organic waste.
- ✓ Best for small spaces but requires care to maintain the right conditions.

3. Compost Bins:

- ✓ Choose a compact bin designed for indoor use.
- ✓ Add a balance of "greens" (food scraps) and "browns" (paper, dry leaves) to avoid odors.

What to Compost:

- Fruit and vegetable peels.
- Coffee grounds and tea bags.
- Eggshells.

What to Avoid:

- Meat, dairy, and oily foods (attract pests).
- Large amounts of citrus (can harm worms in vermicomposting).

Recycling Tips for Urban Dwellers

Recycling is a vital practice, but it's important to do it correctly to ensure materials are actually repurposed.

How to Recycle Effectively:

1. Understand Local Rules: Check your city's recycling guidelines for accepted materials.

2. Clean Your Recyclables: Rinse food containers to prevent contamination.

3. Separate Materials: Remove lids or labels if required by your local program.

4. Drop Off Specialized Items: Batteries, electronics, and lightbulbs often need to be taken to specific recycling centers.

Common Mistakes to Avoid:

1. Recycling items with food residue (e.g., greasy pizza boxes).

2. Placing non-recyclables (like plastic bags) in curbside bins.

Pro Tip: *Use apps like "iRecycle" to locate nearby recycling facilities.*

Reducing Single-Use Plastics

Single-use plastics are among the biggest contributors to urban waste. Transitioning to reusable alternatives is simple and impactful.

Steps to Reduce Plastic Usage:

1. Reusable Bags: Keep cloth bags handy for grocery shopping.

2. Stainless Steel Water Bottles: Replace plastic bottles with durable, refillable ones.

3. Food Storage Alternatives: Use glass containers, silicone wraps, or beeswax wraps instead of plastic wrap.

4. Buy in Bulk: Purchase grains, nuts, and spices in bulk to reduce packaging waste.

Small Changes That Make a Big Difference:

1. Carry reusable utensils and straws when eating out.

2. Choose products with minimal or recyclable packaging.

Impact: If every urban household eliminated single-use plastics, millions of tons of waste could be avoided annually.

Repurposing and Upcycling

Repurposing and upcycling allow you to creatively reuse items, reducing the need to buy new products.

Simple Upcycling Projects:

1. Glass Jars to Storage Containers: Use them to store spices, nuts, or craft supplies.

2. Old T-Shirts to Shopping Bags: Cut and sew unused shirts into reusable bags.

3. Wine Bottles to Décor: Transform bottles into vases, lamps, or candle holders.

4. Wooden Pallets to Furniture: Create shelves, tables, or planters from discarded pallets.

Benefits of Upcycling:

1. Saves money by repurposing materials.

2. Encourages creativity and personalized designs.

3. Reduces landfill waste.

Success Story: *A Toronto-based artist turned discarded textiles into unique fashion pieces, inspiring her community to embrace upcycling.*

Waste reduction isn't just about recycling—it's about rethinking our consumption habits. By composting, recycling responsibly, and repurposing items creatively, you can significantly reduce your impact on the planet while enhancing your urban lifestyle.

Chapter 5:

Eco-Friendly Home Improvements

Energy Efficiency Upgrades

Reducing energy consumption is a key component of sustainable living. Small changes in your home can significantly lower your carbon footprint and energy bills.

1. Switch to LED Lighting

- LED bulbs use up to 75% less energy than traditional incandescent bulbs.
- They last longer, reducing the need for frequent replacements.

2. Install Smart Thermostats

Programmable thermostats help maintain energy efficiency by adjusting heating and cooling based on your schedule.

Example: A smart thermostat can reduce energy costs by up to 10%.

3. Seal Windows and Doors

- Use weatherstripping or caulking to prevent drafts and reduce energy loss.
- Insulated curtains can also help maintain indoor temperatures.

4. Unplug Electronics

Even when off, devices like TVs and chargers consume power. Plug them into power strips and switch off when not in use.

Pro Tip: *Monitor your energy usage with apps or devices like energy meters to identify and address inefficiencies.*

Water-Saving Solutions

Conserving water in urban areas is essential due to high demand and limited resources.

1. Install Low-Flow Fixtures

   - Replace showerheads and faucets with low-flow models to reduce water usage by up to 50%.

2. Fix Leaks Immediately

   - A dripping faucet can waste over 3,000 gallons of water annually.

3. Use Dual-Flush Toilets

   - These systems allow you to choose between a full or partial flush, saving water with every use.

4. Harvest Rainwater

- Set up a small rain barrel on your balcony or near a window to collect water for plants.

5. Efficient Dishwashing and Laundry

- Use full loads when operating dishwashers or washing machines.
- Choose eco-friendly cycles to save both water and energy.

Success Story: *A Melbourne resident reduced their water bill by 30% in a year by combining low-flow fixtures with rainwater harvesting.*

Eco-Friendly Materials and Furniture

Choosing sustainable materials for furniture and home upgrades is both stylish and environmentally responsible.

1. Reclaimed Wood

- Use reclaimed wood for tables, shelves, or flooring.
- It reduces the demand for new timber and gives your space a rustic charm.

2. Bamboo

- A fast-growing and renewable resource, bamboo is ideal for flooring, furniture, and even textiles.

3. Non-Toxic Paints and Finishes

- Choose paints labeled as VOC-free (Volatile Organic Compounds) to improve indoor air quality.

4. Second-Hand Furniture

- Thrift stores, online marketplaces, and estate sales are great places to find unique and affordable pieces.

5. Upcycled Décor

- Repurpose items like old doors into tables or vintage suitcases into storage chests.

Tip: *Look for certifications like FSC (Forest Stewardship Council) to ensure materials are sustainably sourced.*

Indoor Plants for Better Air Quality

Indoor plants not only beautify your space but also act as natural air purifiers.

1. Best Plants for Air Purification:

- ➢ Snake Plant: Removes toxins like formaldehyde and benzene.

- ➢ Spider Plant: Easy to maintain and effective at improving air quality.

- ➢ Peace Lily: Absorbs mold spores and reduces humidity.

2. Create a Green Wall

> ➢ Install a vertical garden indoors to maximize greenery in small spaces.
> ➢ Use herbs like mint or thyme for added functionality.

3. Maintenance Tips:

> ➢ Water moderately to avoid overhydration.
> ➢ Ensure adequate light by placing plants near windows.

Impact: *Studies show that having 2-3 plants per room can reduce airborne toxins by up to 50%.*

Solar and Renewable Energy Solutions

While large-scale solar panels may not be feasible for all urban dwellers, there are small-scale renewable energy solutions for apartment living.

1. Solar-Powered Gadgets

   ➢ Use solar chargers for phones, laptops, and small appliances.
   ➢ Install solar lanterns for balcony or outdoor lighting.

2. Window Solar Panels

   ➢ Compact solar panels can be mounted on windows to generate power for small devices.

3. Community Solar Programs

   ➢ Many urban areas offer shared solar initiatives, where residents buy into a local solar farm and receive credits on their energy bills.

4. Rooftop Gardens with Solar Integration

> Combine rooftop gardening with solar panels for a dual-purpose sustainable setup.

5. Battery Storage

> Store solar energy in compact batteries to use during nighttime or power outages.

Example: *In Tokyo, a resident-powered apartment block uses individual window solar panels to collectively generate energy for shared spaces.*

Eco-friendly home improvements are an investment in your future and the planet's well-being. From simple upgrades like LED bulbs to more advanced solutions like solar gadgets, every step you take reduces your environmental impact while enhancing your living space.

Chapter 6:

Sustainable Transportation

Understanding the Environmental Impact of Transportation

Transportation is one of the largest contributors to greenhouse gas emissions, particularly in urban areas. Shifting to sustainable options can drastically reduce your carbon footprint.

Key Statistics:

- ❖ Road transport contributes nearly 25% of global CO2 emissions.
- ❖ A single car emits approximately 4.6 metric tons of CO2 annually.

How Transportation Choices Affect the Environment:

❖ Fossil Fuels: Gas-powered vehicles rely on non-renewable energy sources, depleting resources and polluting the air.

❖ Congestion: Traffic jams in cities lead to increased idling time, resulting in higher emissions.

Goal: *To transition to transportation modes that minimize environmental harm while meeting daily needs.*

Benefits of Public Transportation

Public transit is one of the most sustainable ways to travel, especially in densely populated urban areas.

Advantages of Public Transportation:

1. Reduced Emissions: Trains and buses emit significantly less CO2 per passenger compared to cars.

2. Energy Efficiency: Mass transit systems use energy more efficiently by transporting many people at once.

3. Cost Savings: Public transit is often cheaper than owning and maintaining a car.

4. Traffic Reduction: Fewer cars on the road mean less congestion and pollution.

How to Utilize Public Transit Effectively:

- ❖ Plan routes using mobile apps to minimize waiting times.
- ❖ Purchase monthly or annual passes for convenience and cost savings.
- ❖ Advocate for improved infrastructure and accessibility in your community.

Embracing Active Transportation

Walking and cycling are the most eco-friendly transportation options. They also offer health and lifestyle benefits.

Benefits of Active Transportation:

1. Zero Emissions: Walking and cycling produce no greenhouse gases.

2. Health Improvements: Regular physical activity reduces the risk of chronic illnesses like heart disease and diabetes.

3. Cost-Free Travel: No fuel, parking, or maintenance expenses.

Tips for Cyclists in Urban Areas:

- ✓ Invest in Safety Gear: Wear helmets, reflective vests, and use lights for visibility.
- ✓ Use Bike Lanes: Stick to designated paths for a safer experience.
- ✓ Secure Your Bike: Use sturdy locks to prevent theft.

Example: *Amsterdam, known for its cycling culture, has over 800,000 bicycles and a network of bike-friendly roads, reducing traffic and emissions.*

Switching to Electric Vehicles (EVs)

For those who need a car, electric vehicles (EVs) are a sustainable alternative to traditional gas-powered cars.

Advantages of EVs:

1. Lower Emissions: EVs produce zero tailpipe emissions and are cleaner overall when charged with renewable energy.

2. Reduced Operating Costs: EVs are cheaper to maintain due to fewer moving parts and lower fuel costs.

3. Government Incentives: Many countries offer tax rebates and subsidies for EV purchases.

Challenges to Consider:

- ✓ Charging Infrastructure: Ensure your city has accessible charging stations.

- ✓ Initial Cost: EVs may have a higher upfront cost, but long-term savings often offset this.

Pro Tip: *Look into shared EV programs or carpooling with electric cars to further reduce costs and emissions.*

Exploring Shared and Micro-Mobility Options

Micro-mobility and shared transportation services are growing in popularity, offering flexible, eco-friendly alternatives.

Shared Mobility Options:

1. Ride-Sharing: Services like Uber and Lyft can reduce the number of cars on the road when shared rides are utilized.

2. Car-Sharing: Platforms like Zipcar allow you to rent a car only when needed, reducing the need for personal vehicle ownership.

Micro-Mobility Solutions:

1. E-Scooters: Electric scooters are ideal for short trips in urban areas.

2. Bike-Sharing: Rent bikes through programs like Citi Bike or Vélib' in major cities.

3. E-Bikes: Electric bicycles provide an energy-efficient option for longer distances with less physical effort.

Benefits of Micro-Mobility:

- ✓ Reduces congestion and emissions.
- ✓ Offers affordable and accessible transportation for short distances.
- ✓ Encourages a shift away from car dependency.

Example: *In Paris, the Vélib' bike-sharing program has reduced traffic congestion and provided residents with an eco-friendly travel option.*

Sustainable transportation isn't just about reducing emissions—it's about embracing healthier, more efficient, and cost-effective ways of moving through the city. Whether it's taking public transit, cycling, or switching to an EV, every step toward greener transportation contributes to a cleaner, more sustainable urban environment. Next chapter will discuss sustainable consumption

Chapter 7:

Sustainable Shopping and Consumption

Understanding Sustainable Consumption

Sustainable consumption involves purchasing goods that have minimal environmental impact and support ethical practices. This requires mindful decisions about what we buy and how we use resources.

What Is Sustainable Shopping?

- Eco-Friendly Products: Items made with minimal environmental damage.

- Ethical Sourcing: Supporting brands that ensure fair wages and safe working conditions for workers.
- Minimalism: Buying less and prioritizing quality over quantity.

The Environmental Impact of Overconsumption:

- Fast fashion alone contributes to 10% of global carbon emissions.
- Plastics used in packaging often end up in oceans, harming marine life.

Goal: *To shift from a "consume and discard" culture to one of thoughtful, sustainable consumption.*

How to Shop Sustainably

1. Buy Locally:

   ✓ Supporting local businesses reduces transportation emissions and boosts the local economy.
   ✓ Farmers' markets are a great place to find fresh, organic, and seasonal produce.

2. Choose Reusable over Disposable:

   ✓ Opt for reusable bags, water bottles, and coffee cups instead of single-use plastics.

3. Look for Certifications:

   ✓ Labels like Fair Trade, Organic, and FSC (Forest Stewardship Council) ensure sustainable practices.

4. Support Sustainable Brands:

- ✓ Research brands that prioritize eco-friendly materials, ethical labor, and transparency.

5. Avoid Impulse Purchases:

- ✓ Before buying, ask yourself if the item is truly necessary and how long it will last.

Pro Tip: *Create a shopping list to stay focused and avoid unnecessary purchases.*

Sustainable Fashion Choices

Fast fashion has become a major environmental issue, but there are ways to dress sustainably without compromising style.

1. Opt for Second-Hand Clothing:

Thrift stores, consignment shops, and online platforms like Poshmark offer affordable, stylish options.

2. Invest in Quality Over Quantity:

High-quality garments last longer, reducing the need for frequent replacements.

3. Embrace Capsule Wardrobes:

Build a wardrobe with versatile, timeless pieces that can be mixed and matched.

4. Repair and Repurpose:

Extend the life of your clothes by repairing minor damages or repurposing old items into new styles.

5. Choose Sustainable Fabrics:

Look for natural, biodegradable materials like organic cotton, hemp, or bamboo.

Avoid synthetic fabrics like polyester, which shed microplastics during washing.

Example: A New York-based sustainable fashion brand turned discarded plastic bottles into high-quality activewear, demonstrating innovative recycling practices.

Reducing Food Waste While Shopping

Food waste is a significant environmental issue, but smart shopping habits can help minimize it.

1. Plan Your Meals:

Create a weekly meal plan to avoid buying unnecessary ingredients.

Stick to your grocery list to reduce impulse purchases.

2. Buy in Bulk:

Purchase grains, spices, and non-perishables in bulk to save on packaging and cost.

Use reusable containers to store bulk items.

3. Choose "Ugly" Produce:

Many fruits and vegetables are discarded due to cosmetic imperfections. Supporting "imperfect" produce reduces waste.

4. Support Zero-Waste Stores:

These stores offer package-free products, encouraging customers to bring their own containers.

5. Understand Expiry Dates:

"Best before" dates are often guidelines, not mandates. Use your senses to determine if food is still edible.

Tip: Apps like "Too Good To Go" help you buy surplus food from restaurants and stores at discounted rates.

Adopting a Mindful Consumer Mindset

Mindful consumption goes beyond shopping habits—it's about changing your overall approach to consumerism.

1. Buy Less, Choose Wisely:

Ask yourself if a purchase aligns with your values of sustainability and minimalism.

2. Focus on Longevity:

Invest in products designed to last, from electronics to home goods.

3. Learn to DIY:

Make your own cleaning products, grow herbs at home, or upcycle old items into something new.

4. Educate Yourself:

Stay informed about the environmental impact of various industries and products.

Follow blogs, podcasts, or social media accounts dedicated to sustainable living.

5. Share and Borrow:

Use community platforms to borrow tools, share books, or exchange unused items with others.

Example: A neighborhood in San Francisco started a tool-sharing library, reducing the need for residents to buy rarely-used tools.

To sum up, sustainable shopping and consumption require a shift in mindset, but the rewards are immense—for the planet and your personal well-being. By making intentional choices, you can reduce waste, support ethical practices, and create a ripple effect of positive change in your community.

Chapter 8:

Building a Green Community

The Power of Community in Sustainability

Creating a sustainable urban environment isn't just about individual actions; it's about fostering a collective effort. Communities play a crucial role in promoting environmental consciousness, sharing resources, and advocating for green initiatives.

Why Community Matters in Sustainability:

Shared Resources: Communities can pool resources for greater environmental impact, such as car-sharing programs or community gardens.

Stronger Advocacy: Collective action is more effective when advocating for policy changes, like improved recycling programs or green building regulations.

Knowledge Sharing: People learn from each other and spread ideas about sustainable practices through community engagement.

Goal: To build a community where sustainability is a shared value, creating both immediate and long-term environmental benefits.

2: Creating Community Gardens

Urban gardening not only beautifies neighborhoods but also provides fresh, locally grown produce, which can reduce the carbon footprint of food transportation.

Steps to Start a Community Garden:

1. Find a Suitable Location: Look for vacant lots, parks, or unused spaces in the neighborhood.

2. Gather Support: Engage with local residents to get their support and involvement. Hold informational meetings to generate interest.

3. Organize Gardening Plots: Designate individual plots for families or groups, or create communal spaces for shared planting.

4. Choose Sustainable Gardening Practices: Use organic gardening methods, such as composting,

avoiding synthetic pesticides, and using water-efficient irrigation systems.

Benefits of Community Gardens:

Improves access to healthy, fresh food.

Fosters stronger neighborhood bonds.

Promotes biodiversity and reduces urban heat island effects.

Success Story: In Detroit, abandoned urban areas have been transformed into thriving community gardens, providing food and community empowerment.

3: Organizing Local Clean-Up Initiatives

Clean-up events can improve the environmental health of urban areas while fostering community spirit. These efforts can focus on cleaning parks, streets, or local waterways.

How to Organize a Clean-Up Event:

1. Choose a Location: Select a public area in need of attention, such as a park, beach, or riverbank.

2. Set a Date: Pick a weekend or holiday to maximize volunteer participation.

3. Gather Supplies: Provide gloves, trash bags, recycling bins, and other necessary materials.

4. Promote the Event: Use social media, local bulletin boards, and word-of-mouth to recruit participants.

5. Ensure Proper Waste Disposal: Sort collected materials for recycling, composting, or disposal according to local guidelines.

Impact of Clean-Up Initiatives:

Reduces pollution and enhances the beauty of public spaces.

Promotes environmental awareness among participants.

Provides an opportunity for local businesses and schools to get involved.

Example: The "Trash Tag Challenge" has gained popularity on social media, encouraging people around the world to clean up public spaces, with some urban areas organizing large-scale community events.

4: Supporting Local Sustainability Initiatives

Getting involved in local sustainability projects and supporting eco-friendly initiatives helps amplify the impact of green movements in your community.

Types of Local Sustainability Projects to Support:

1. Urban Green Spaces: Advocate for parks, tree planting, and green roofs to improve air quality and biodiversity.

2. Renewable Energy Projects: Support initiatives like community solar power or wind energy programs.

3. Eco-Friendly Public Transport: Encourage the development of bike lanes, electric buses, and expanded metro services.

4. Waste Reduction Programs: Participate in or promote community-wide recycling and composting efforts.

Ways to Get Involved:

Attend local government meetings to voice support for sustainable policies.

Volunteer with environmental non-profits.

Start a petition for green initiatives in your neighborhood.

Example: In Portland, Oregon, residents work with the city to promote the installation of green roofs on commercial buildings, reducing energy consumption and managing stormwater runoff.

5: Building a Sustainable Mindset Through Education and Outreach

Sustainability becomes ingrained in the community when people understand the value of environmental responsibility. Education and outreach initiatives are key to fostering a culture of sustainability.

Steps to Educate Your Community:

1. Workshops and Events: Organize talks or workshops on topics such as composting, sustainable living, or environmental activism.

2. Collaborate with Local Schools: Partner with local schools to integrate sustainability into the curriculum and organize youth-focused eco-events.

3. Create Green Resources: Develop a community newsletter, website, or social media   dedicated to sustainability tips and local green events.

4. Encourage Sustainable Practices: Advocate for zero-waste practices, like reducing plastic use and

minimizing food waste, in local businesses and schools.

Success Story: *In Copenhagen, the city government collaborates with local organizations to host sustainability workshops that reach thousands of residents each year, helping the city become one of the greenest in the world.*

Building a green community is not a single-person effort; it requires collaboration, commitment, and shared vision. By coming together, you can create an environment where sustainable practices thrive, benefiting not only the local ecosystem but also the health and well-being of everyone who lives there.

Chapter 9:

Overcoming Challenges in Sustainable Living

1: Common Barriers to Sustainable Living

Living sustainably can often seem challenging, especially when faced with societal norms, economic limitations, and lifestyle habits that contradict environmental goals. However, understanding these obstacles is the first step toward overcoming them.

Key Challenges:

1. Cost of Sustainable Products: Eco-friendly alternatives can be more expensive than conventional products.

2. Convenience and Accessibility: Sustainable options like zero-waste stores or public transportation may not be readily available in every area.

3. Lack of Awareness: Many people are unaware of the impact of their daily habits on the environment or lack knowledge on how to make sustainable choices.

4. Cultural and Social Norms: The prevailing culture often prioritizes convenience, consumption, and instant gratification over sustainability.

Goal: To identify these barriers and develop strategies to make sustainable living accessible, affordable, and achievable for everyone.

2: Overcoming the Cost Barrier

While sustainable products can sometimes have a higher initial price, the long-term savings and environmental benefits often outweigh the extra cost.

Strategies to Overcome High Costs:

1. Buy in Bulk: Purchasing products like grains, cleaning supplies, and toiletries in bulk can reduce cost per unit and packaging waste.

2. Invest in Quality: Higher-quality items, such as durable clothing or energy-efficient appliances, often last longer, reducing the need for frequent replacements.

3. DIY Solutions: Making your own products, such as cleaning supplies, composting bins, or beauty products, can be significantly cheaper than buying pre-made, eco-friendly alternatives.

4. Seek Out Discounts and Subsidies: Many cities offer incentives for purchasing sustainable products like electric vehicles or solar panels. Look for local programs or discounts on eco-friendly items.

5. Second-Hand and Upcycling: Thrift stores, online marketplaces, and upcycling help you acquire goods at a lower cost, often with a smaller environmental footprint.

Pro Tip: Consider the long-term savings of sustainable choices, such as reduced energy bills or less frequent replacements, when weighing initial costs.

3: Making Sustainable Living Convenient

Convenience is a significant barrier to sustainable living, especially in urban environments. However, small shifts in habits and accessible alternatives can help integrate sustainability into your daily routine.

Ways to Increase Convenience:

1. Utilize Mobile Apps: Use apps like Recycle Coach to find recycling information, Too Good To Go to buy discounted surplus food, or Bike Map to locate bike lanes and trails.

2. Buy Online with Eco-Friendly Options: Choose retailers that use minimal packaging or offer carbon-neutral shipping options.

3. Opt for Local Services: Find local, sustainable services like composting programs, zero-waste stores, or repair shops that offer convenient, eco-friendly alternatives.

4. Create a Green Routine: Set up systems that make sustainable practices easy—such as keeping reusable bags in your car or a compost bin in your kitchen.

5. Community Resources: If certain sustainable options aren't available in your area, see if there's interest in establishing new resources, such as a

neighborhood tool-sharing program or a carpooling system.

Example: In cities like Berlin and San Francisco, shared mobility services, such as electric scooters and bikes, have made it easier for residents to get around without needing a car.

Educating and Inspiring Others

Lack of awareness is often a barrier to sustainable living. By sharing knowledge and motivating others, you can help shift attitudes and behaviors in your community.

Ways to Spread Awareness and Inspire Change:

1. Host Workshops or Events: Organize community events, like a DIY zero-waste workshop or a sustainable living fair, to share tips and resources.

2. Lead by Example: Adopt sustainable habits, such as using reusable bags, reducing food waste, or carpooling, and share your experiences with others.

3. Social Media and Blogging: Use social media to post about sustainable practices or start a blog to engage a larger audience with environmental tips.

4. Collaborate with Local Businesses: Work with local restaurants, shops, or schools to introduce sustainable initiatives, such as offering discounts

for reusable containers or hosting a recycling drive.

5. Advocate for Change: Support environmental campaigns or write letters to local policymakers to promote sustainable practices on a larger scale.

Example: In New Zealand, a growing community of "sustainability influencers" has used social media platforms to raise awareness about waste reduction, eco-friendly fashion, and more, leading to widespread behavior changes.

5: Overcoming Social and Cultural Norms

In many societies, the dominant culture prioritizes convenience, consumerism, and short-term gratification over environmental well-being. Changing these social and cultural norms requires persistent effort and collective action.

Strategies to Shift Cultural Norms:

1. Promote the Social Benefits of Sustainability: Emphasize how sustainable living can lead to healthier lifestyles, stronger communities, and lower costs.

2. Normalize Eco-Friendly Practices: Encourage behaviors such as recycling, composting, and using public transportation so they become mainstream rather than niche.

3. Support Policy Changes: Advocate for policies that encourage sustainability, such as urban farming initiatives, better waste management systems, and government incentives for green businesses.

4. Celebrate Successes: Recognize and celebrate communities, businesses, and individuals who are making a difference. This can help inspire others to follow suit.

5. Create Sustainable Social Spaces: Organize events, from sustainable potlucks to green art shows, that bring people together to celebrate eco-conscious living.

Example: In Sweden, a strong cultural focus on sustainability has led to widespread adoption of eco-friendly policies, including energy-efficient public transportation and national recycling programs.

Overcoming the challenges of sustainable living may not always be easy, but each barrier presents an opportunity for growth, innovation, and change. By staying committed to making sustainable choices, advocating for others, and fostering a supportive environment, we can collectively create a more sustainable future for all.

Chapter 10:

The Future of Urban Sustainability

1: The Growing Importance of Sustainable Cities

As urban populations continue to rise globally, the need for sustainable cities has never been more pressing. Urban areas are responsible for a large portion of the world's carbon emissions, waste, and resource consumption. However, cities also offer a unique opportunity for innovation and positive environmental change, serving as testing grounds for sustainable solutions that can be scaled worldwide.

Why Focus on Urban Sustainability?

Urbanization Trends: By 2050, nearly 70% of the world's population is projected to live in cities, leading to increased demand for resources.

Environmental Impact: Cities account for about 70% of global energy consumption and contribute to more than 60% of greenhouse gas emissions.

Economic and Social Benefits: Green cities tend to be more resilient to climate change, economically efficient, and provide a higher quality of life for residents.

Goal: To create cities that are environmentally sustainable, economically vibrant, and socially inclusive, reducing the environmental footprint while improving the well-being of urban dwellers.

2: Key Innovations in Urban Sustainability

Urban sustainability is driven by technological advancements and creative solutions that address both environmental and social challenges. Below are some of the key innovations shaping the future of sustainable cities.

1. Green Building and Sustainable Architecture:

Green buildings are designed to minimize energy use, reduce waste, and promote indoor environmental quality. Features include solar panels, green roofs, and passive heating and cooling systems.

Smart buildings, which use IoT (Internet of Things) technology, optimize energy use by adjusting heating, cooling, and lighting in real-time based on occupancy and weather.

2. Urban Agriculture and Vertical Farming:

Vertical farming uses skyscrapers or multi-story buildings to grow crops, reducing the need for arable land and minimizing transportation emissions.

Urban gardens, rooftop farms, and community gardens help cities grow their own food, improving food security and reducing food waste.

3. Renewable Energy Integration:

Cities are increasingly integrating renewable energy sources like solar, wind, and geothermal to power homes and businesses. Many urban areas are adopting district-wide solar power systems, where entire neighborhoods are powered by shared solar grids.

4. Smart Mobility and Electric Transportation:

Electric cars, buses, and bicycles reduce greenhouse gas emissions and air pollution. The rise of autonomous vehicles and shared mobility services (e.g., ride-sharing, carpooling) are also helping to reduce congestion and emissions.

Bike-sharing programs and electric scooters are transforming urban transportation, offering efficient and eco-friendly options for short-distance travel.

3: Urban Waste Management and Circular Economy

A sustainable urban future also hinges on rethinking how we manage waste. Traditional linear models of "take, make, dispose" are giving way to the circular economy, where products and materials are reused, repaired, and recycled, rather than discarded.

1. Zero-Waste Initiatives:

Cities like San Francisco have made significant strides toward zero-waste goals, encouraging residents and businesses to recycle, compost, and reduce waste.

Waste-to-Energy: Cities are exploring ways to convert waste into energy through processes like anaerobic digestion or waste incineration, further reducing landfill use.

2. Composting and Urban Farming:

Community composting programs allow residents to turn organic waste into nutrient-rich soil, supporting urban agriculture and reducing methane emissions from landfills.

Composting also reduces the need for chemical fertilizers, which can pollute water sources.

3. Extended Producer Responsibility (EPR):

Under EPR policies, manufacturers are held accountable for the end-of-life disposal of their products, ensuring that waste is minimized and recycling is maximized.

4. Smart Waste Management:

Smart waste bins with sensors that monitor fill levels help optimize collection routes and improve efficiency. Some cities are adopting "pay-as-you-throw" systems, where residents pay based on the amount of waste they generate, encouraging waste reduction.

4: Nature-Based Solutions and Green Infrastructure

Integrating nature into urban spaces is an essential component of making cities more sustainable. Nature-based solutions (NbS) harness the power of ecosystems to address urban challenges, such as water management, air pollution, and climate change adaptation.

1. Green Roofs and Urban Forests:

Green roofs provide insulation, reduce energy costs, and absorb rainwater, mitigating flooding risks.

Urban forests and tree canopies help cool cities, reduce air pollution, and provide habitats for biodiversity, improving overall urban health. These natural interventions not only enhance the aesthetic appeal of cities but also contribute to the physical and mental well-being of their residents. Urban forests, in particular, act as carbon sinks, offsetting emissions and creating a more breathable environment.

Permeable Surfaces and Rain Gardens:

Replacing impermeable surfaces like concrete with permeable materials allows rainwater to infiltrate the ground, reducing urban flooding and replenishing groundwater. Rain gardens are another effective nature-based solution. They are designed to absorb and filter stormwater, enhancing water quality while adding greenery to urban areas.

Wetlands and Coastal Resilience:

Restoring wetlands in urban and peri-urban areas helps to regulate water cycles, prevent flooding, and improve water quality. In coastal cities, green infrastructure such as mangroves and salt marshes acts as a buffer against storm surges and sea-level rise, protecting communities while preserving natural ecosystems.

Community Involvement and Co-Benefits:

Successful implementation of nature-based solutions requires the active participation of local communities. By involving residents in the planning and maintenance of green infrastructure, cities can foster a sense of ownership and encourage sustainable practices. Moreover, these projects often provide additional benefits, such as job creation, recreational spaces, and improved public health.

Incorporating nature into urban planning is not merely a trend but a necessity for achieving sustainable development goals. By prioritizing NbS, cities can build resilience against environmental challenges while enhancing the quality of urban life for generations to come.

Conclusion:

A Greener Future for Urban Dwellers

As we've explored throughout this guide, sustainable living in urban environments is not only possible, but also increasingly necessary. Cities, which house more than half of the world's population, are at the forefront of the fight against climate change. Their dense populations, high resource consumption, and significant environmental impact demand innovative solutions. However, they also present a unique opportunity for transformative change, where technological advancements, community engagement, and policy reform can lead to more sustainable, livable spaces for all.

Key Takeaways from This Guide:

1. Sustainability Starts with the Individual: Small, everyday choices—such as reducing waste, conserving energy, and supporting eco-friendly businesses—add up to make a significant difference.

2. Community Engagement is Essential: Sustainability is not just about individual actions; it thrives when communities work together, share resources, and support local green initiatives.

3. Urban Spaces Can Be Green Spaces: From community gardens to green roofs, cities have

immense potential to integrate nature into their infrastructure, improving both the environment and the quality of life for residents.

4. Innovation is the Key to Sustainable Cities: From renewable energy adoption to smart waste management and sustainable architecture, innovation is driving the future of urban sustainability.

5. The Role of Policy: Effective governance is vital to creating and maintaining sustainable cities. Policies that encourage green building, renewable energy, and sustainable transportation are crucial for long-term success.

A Call to Action:

As an urban dweller, you have the power to influence change—whether through the choices you make in your daily life or by joining a larger movement within your community. Together, we can reshape the future of our cities, making them healthier, more resilient, and environmentally friendly for generations to come.

Sustainability is not a far-off goal but a practical and achievable reality. By taking actionable steps today, you can contribute to the global effort of building cities that are not only green but also thriving, equitable, and sustainable.

The future of urban sustainability is in our hands. Let's get started, one small change at a time.

This concludes the guide on "Sustainable Living for Urban Dwellers." If you're inspired to take the next step or explore more specific areas of sustainability, there are countless resources, communities, and actions waiting for you. The journey toward a greener urban lifestyle begins now.